The Might of a Woman

The main Strength and Power of a Woman

Table of contents

Introduction

The Might of a Woman

In a world shaped by diverse narratives and evolving societal norms, the empowerment and strength of women have emerged as pivotal themes. The might of a woman transcends conventional stereotypes, encompassing a multifaceted spectrum of resilience, leadership, and influence. This introspective exploration seeks to unravel the intricate layers that constitute the formidable force behind women's might, acknowledging the historical struggles, celebrating achievements, and envisioning a future where the true potential of women is fully recognized.

Historically, women have confronted systemic barriers that restricted their opportunities and hindered the realization of their capabilities. From suffragettes fighting for the right to vote to trailblazing individuals breaking gender norms in various fields, the journey towards recognizing the might of women has been marked by tenacity and perseverance. Despite facing adversity, women have consistently demonstrated unwavering strength, challenging societal expectations and carving out spaces for themselves in realms previously dominated by men.

The might of a woman is intricately tied to her resilience in the face of adversity. Across cultures and time periods, women have borne the weight of societal expectations, navigating challenges with grace and determination. Whether shouldering the responsibilities of caregiving, overcoming gender-based discrimination, or confronting systemic inequalities, women have consistently exhibited a resilience that forms the bedrock of their might. This resilience extends beyond individual experiences to encompass collective movements that have shaped the course of history, emphasizing the power of solidarity among women in their pursuit of equality and justice.

Leadership, a facet of the might of a woman, has witnessed a paradigm shift as women continue to ascend to positions of influence across various sectors. Breaking through the proverbial glass ceiling, women leaders bring a unique perspective to decision-making, fostering diversity and innovation. The might of women in leadership is not only about individual achievements but also about challenging traditional hierarchies and creating more inclusive spaces where diverse voices are heard and valued.

Furthermore, the might of a woman is evident in her ability to nurture and catalyze change within communities. Women often play a pivotal role in shaping the values and well-being of families and societies. As educators, caregivers, and community builders, women contribute to the fabric of society in ways that extend far beyond conventional metrics of success. Their impact is felt in the resilience they instill in future generations, the compassion they demonstrate in times of crisis, and the transformative influence they exert on the social and cultural landscapes.

Acknowledging the might of a woman also requires an examination of the cultural shifts and changing narratives that contribute to redefining gender roles. As societies evolve, the perception of women's strength transcends traditional stereotypes, embracing a more inclusive understanding that recognizes and celebrates the diversity of women's experiences. The breaking down of rigid gender norms allows for a more authentic expression of individual identity and strength, empowering women to chart their own paths and contribute to a more equitable world.

Looking forward, envisioning the might of a woman involves fostering environments that empower women to reach their full potential. This necessitates dismantling remaining barriers to equality, advocating for policies that promote inclusivity, and fostering a culture that values and amplifies the voices of women. As technological advancements and global connectivity continue to reshape the world, the active participation of women in all spheres becomes not just a matter of justice but a strategic imperative for societal progress.

In conclusion, the might of a woman is a dynamic and multifaceted force that encompasses resilience, leadership, and the ability to catalyze positive change. This introspective journey invites a deeper understanding of the historical struggles, the present achievements, and the future possibilities that define the strength of women. As societies evolve, recognizing and amplifying the might of women becomes not only a moral imperative but a strategic investment in a more just, equitable, and prosperous future for all.

Defining Female Strength

Defining female strength encompasses a multifaceted exploration of the qualities, experiences, and resilience that characterize the women who navigate the diverse landscapes of life. It goes beyond conventional notions, challenging stereotypes and embracing the richness of individual narratives.

Strength, for women, is rooted in the ability to confront adversity with resilience and determination. It transcends physical might, extending into emotional fortitude and intellectual prowess. In a world that often imposes rigid expectations on women, understanding and celebrating the depth of female strength is crucial.

One aspect of female strength lies in the ability to navigate societal expectations and break through traditional roles. Women have historically been confined to predefined roles, but the contemporary landscape witnesses a paradigm shift. Female strength emerges as women challenge stereotypes, pursue education and careers, and assert their agency in shaping their destinies.

The strength of women is evident in their capacity to balance diverse roles. Juggling careers, family responsibilities, and personal aspirations requires a unique blend of resilience and adaptability. This ability to multitask and find equilibrium is a testament to the strength that women bring to various aspects of their lives.

Furthermore, emotional intelligence forms a cornerstone of female strength. Women often excel in understanding and navigating complex emotions, fostering connections, and building supportive communities. This emotional strength not only enables women to nurture relationships but also empowers them to empathize with diverse perspectives, fostering a more compassionate and inclusive society.

Female strength also manifests in the face of adversity. Many women have overcome formidable challenges, ranging from systemic inequalities to personal hardships. Their stories echo the resilience that defines the essence of female strength, proving that setbacks can be catalysts for growth rather than impediments.

The concept of defining female strength also involves dispelling the myth that vulnerability is a sign of weakness. Acknowledging vulnerabilities, expressing emotions, and seeking support are integral components of strength. The ability to be vulnerable, to ask for help when needed, is a courageous act that adds depth and authenticity to the portrayal of female strength.

Moreover, the intersectionality of female strength emphasizes the importance of recognizing and embracing diversity. Women from various backgrounds, ethnicities, and cultures bring unique strengths shaped by their distinct experiences. An inclusive understanding of female strength acknowledges and celebrates this diversity, fostering a more equitable and empowering narrative.

In the realm of education, female strength is evident in the increasing representation of women in STEM fields, leadership positions, and other traditionally male-dominated spheres. Breaking through these barriers requires resilience, determination, and a commitment to dismantling gender biases that persist in various sectors.

The portrayal of female strength in media and popular culture plays a crucial role in shaping societal perceptions. Moving away from one-dimensional stereotypes, authentic representations of women in all their complexity contribute to a more nuanced understanding of female strength. Celebrating women who challenge norms, pursue their passions, and contribute to their communities showcases the diverse facets of female strength.

Furthermore, reproductive choices and autonomy are integral aspects of defining female strength. The ability to make decisions about one's body, reproductive health, and family planning is a fundamental expression of agency. Recognizing and respecting these choices as acts of strength contributes to dismantling patriarchal norms that seek to control women's bodies and lives.
In the workplace, advocating for gender equality and breaking through the glass ceiling exemplify female strength. Women who navigate professional challenges, challenge biases, and contribute to creating inclusive work environments pave the way for future generations. Addressing wage gaps, promoting mentorship, and fostering a culture of support are essential components of defining female strength in the professional sphere.

In conclusion, defining female strength requires a holistic and inclusive perspective that goes beyond stereotypes and embraces the richness of women's experiences. It involves acknowledging the myriad ways in which women exhibit resilience, intelligence, emotional depth, and the courage to challenge societal norms. By dismantling stereotypes, celebrating diversity, and recognizing the strength inherent in vulnerability, society can contribute to a more empowering and equitable narrative of female strength.

Physical Strength

The physical strength of a woman is a multifaceted and empowering aspect that goes beyond conventional stereotypes. Breaking free from traditional expectations, women across the globe showcase remarkable physical prowess, challenging preconceived notions about gender and strength. This strength is not solely defined by brute force but encompasses resilience, endurance, and adaptability.

One aspect of a woman's physical strength is evident in her muscular structure. Contrary to outdated beliefs, women possess the capacity to develop and maintain significant muscle mass. Strength training, a key component of fitness, allows women to build and tone muscles, contributing to their overall physical strength. This strength isn't just for aesthetic purposes; it enhances daily functionality, supporting activities ranging from lifting groceries to participating in sports.

Moreover, women exhibit exceptional strength in endurance activities. Endurance is not limited to marathons or long-distance races; it permeates everyday life. Women often navigate demanding schedules, balancing work, family, and personal commitments. This ability to sustain physical and mental effort over extended periods reflects a unique form of strength, demonstrating resilience and determination.

Pregnancy and childbirth underscore another dimension of a woman's physical strength. The female body undergoes remarkable transformations during pregnancy, adapting to support the growing life within. Labor and childbirth are intense physical experiences that demand immense strength. The endurance displayed during this process is a testament to the incredible capabilities of the female body.

Beyond the physical, a woman's strength is intertwined with emotional resilience. Facing societal pressures, stereotypes, and gender biases, women often overcome adversity with grace and tenacity. The ability to navigate challenges, whether personal or professional, requires a unique blend of mental fortitude and emotional strength.

In the realm of sports, female athletes continually shatter records and redefine expectations. From Serena Williams in tennis to Simone Biles in gymnastics, women showcase unparalleled physical prowess, proving that athleticism knows no gender boundaries. These athletes inspire and empower, challenging perceptions of what women can achieve in the realm of physical performance.

Furthermore, women's strength extends to mental and emotional well-being. The capacity to manage stress, multitask, and maintain emotional equilibrium in the face of various pressures exemplifies a formidable strength. Women often excel in roles requiring empathy, communication, and emotional intelligence, showcasing a diverse range of strengths that contribute to both personal and professional success.

The concept of physical strength in women also encompasses adaptability. Women frequently navigate various life stages, from puberty to menopause, each bringing its own set of physical changes. The ability to adapt to these changes and maintain a sense of strength and self-confidence is a testament to the resilience inherent in women.

It is essential to recognize that physical strength in women is not a one-size-fits-all attribute. Each woman's journey is unique, and her strength may manifest in different ways. Embracing diversity in expressions of strength fosters a more inclusive and empowering narrative for women.

In conclusion, the physical strength of a woman is a multifaceted and empowering quality that extends far beyond conventional stereotypes. From muscular strength and endurance to the unique challenges of pregnancy and childbirth, women continually demonstrate remarkable physical prowess. Their strength encompasses emotional resilience, mental fortitude, and adaptability, challenging societal norms and inspiring future generations. Recognizing and celebrating the diverse expressions of strength in women contributes to a more inclusive and empowering narrative for all.

Emotional Strength

Emotional strength in women is a multifaceted and empowering attribute that transcends societal norms and stereotypes. It is a quality that manifests in various forms, shaping the way women navigate challenges, express vulnerability, and cultivate resilience in the face of adversity.

One aspect of a woman's emotional strength lies in her ability to embrace vulnerability. Contrary to the misconception that strength is synonymous with stoicism, a woman's emotional fortitude often thrives when she allows herself to be open and authentic about her emotions. By acknowledging vulnerability, women can connect with others on a deeper level, fostering empathy and understanding in relationships.

Furthermore, the emotional strength of women is evident in their resilience amidst life's inevitable hardships. Whether grappling with personal setbacks, professional challenges, or societal expectations, women often display remarkable perseverance. This resilience is not born out of an absence of pain but rather from the courage to confront and overcome it, demonstrating a tenacity that inspires those around them.

The capacity for empathy is another dimension of emotional strength that women frequently embody. The ability to understand and share the feelings of others not only fosters meaningful connections but also contributes to a more compassionate and empathetic society. Women, often nurturing by nature, play a pivotal role in creating a support system where emotional understanding is prioritized.

Moreover, a woman's emotional strength is intertwined with her capacity for self-love and self-compassion. In a world that can be harsh and critical, women who possess emotional strength cultivate a positive relationship with themselves. This self-love serves as a foundation for overall well-being, allowing women to navigate challenges with a sense of self-worth and confidence.

The empowerment of women's emotional strength is also closely linked to their ability to express a range of emotions authentically. Societal norms have historically confined women to specific emotional roles, but as societal perspectives evolve, women are increasingly empowered to embrace the full spectrum of their feelings. This authenticity not only strengthens their own emotional well-being but also challenges stereotypes, contributing to a more inclusive understanding of femininity.

Additionally, the emotional strength of women is evident in their adeptness at forming and maintaining meaningful connections. Whether in familial, platonic, or romantic relationships, women often excel at creating supportive networks. This ability to foster connections is rooted in emotional intelligence, allowing women to navigate complex interpersonal dynamics with grace and understanding.

Furthermore, women's emotional strength is a catalyst for personal growth and self-discovery. Through introspection and a willingness to confront uncomfortable truths, women develop a profound understanding of themselves. This self-awareness empowers them to make informed decisions, set boundaries, and pursue paths aligned with their authentic selves.

In the professional sphere, emotional strength equips women with the resilience needed to navigate gender biases and overcome systemic challenges. Breaking through glass ceilings and defying expectations, women demonstrate that emotional strength is not a hindrance but an asset that propels them forward in diverse fields.

It is crucial to recognize that emotional strength in women is not a uniform trait but a diverse spectrum shaped by individual experiences, backgrounds, and personalities. The intersectionality of factors such as race, ethnicity, socioeconomic status, and more, further enriches the tapestry of emotional strength within the female experience.

In conclusion, the emotional strength of women is a powerful force that defies stereotypes and contributes to the overall resilience and well-being of individuals and society. From embracing vulnerability and resilience to fostering empathy and forming meaningful connections, women's emotional strength is a dynamic and empowering quality that shapes their experiences and influences the world around them.

Advocacy and Activism

Advocacy and activism are powerful tools for driving social and political change, each playing a distinct yet interconnected role in shaping the world we live in. Advocacy involves speaking or acting on behalf of a cause or issue, while activism encompasses a broader range of activities aimed at creating awareness, mobilizing communities, and effecting change. Together, these forces serve as catalysts for progress, challenging established norms and fostering a more just and equitable society.

At its core, advocacy is about giving a voice to the voiceless. It involves individuals or groups championing a particular cause, seeking to influence policies, practices, or public opinion. Advocates may use various channels, such as lobbying, public speaking, or media campaigns, to convey their message and garner support. The goal is to bring attention to issues ranging from human rights violations to environmental concerns, with the ultimate aim of fostering positive change.

One notable aspect of advocacy is its ability to bridge gaps between those affected by an issue and decision-makers. Advocates often serve as intermediaries, translating the concerns of marginalized or oppressed communities into language that resonates with policymakers. This translation is crucial for fostering understanding and empathy, as it helps decision-makers recognize the human impact of their choices.

Activism, on the other hand, is a more encompassing term that includes a spectrum of actions taken to bring about change. Activists are individuals or groups committed to challenging the status quo and addressing social, political, or environmental issues. Activism can take various forms, ranging from peaceful protests and civil disobedience to community organizing and online campaigns.

The power of activism lies in its ability to disrupt complacency and demand attention. Whether it's through large-scale marches, sit-ins, or grassroots movements, activists strive to create a visible and undeniable presence that forces society to confront pressing issues. Activism often goes hand in hand with advocacy, as both share the common goal of effecting positive change.

One key element of successful advocacy and activism is strategic communication. Crafting compelling narratives and messages is essential for capturing the public's attention and mobilizing support. Utilizing various media platforms, including social media, enables advocates and activists to reach broader audiences and amplify their message. The ability to tell a compelling story can turn a complex issue into a relatable and urgent cause, inspiring individuals to join the movement for change.

Moreover, technology has transformed the landscape of advocacy and activism. The advent of social media platforms has democratized communication, providing a platform for individuals to share their stories, connect with like-minded activists, and organize events. Hashtags, viral campaigns, and online petitions have become powerful tools for raising awareness and rallying support for causes.

However, the digital realm also poses challenges, as misinformation and echo chambers can hinder constructive dialogue. Navigating the online space requires a nuanced approach, emphasizing fact-checking, collaboration, and inclusivity to ensure that advocacy efforts remain credible and effective.

Intersectionality plays a crucial role in both advocacy and activism. Recognizing the interconnectedness of various social issues, advocates and activists strive to address the overlapping and intersecting forms of discrimination and oppression that individuals may face. By adopting an intersectional approach, movements become more inclusive and better equipped to dismantle systemic injustices.

In the pursuit of change, advocates and activists often encounter resistance from those who benefit from the existing power structures. Overcoming this resistance requires resilience, strategic thinking, and a commitment to long-term goals. Collaborative efforts, alliances, and solidarity among diverse groups strengthen the collective impact of advocacy and activism.

History is replete with examples of successful advocacy and activism leading to transformative change. The civil rights movement in the United States, the women's suffrage movement, and the anti-apartheid movement in South Africa are just a few instances where tireless advocacy and activism played pivotal roles in dismantling oppressive systems. While progress has been made in many areas, contemporary challenges demand continued advocacy and activism. Global issues such as climate change, inequality, and systemic discrimination persist, necessitating sustained efforts to effect meaningful change. The urgency of these challenges underscores the importance of advocacy and activism as indispensable tools for shaping a more just and sustainable future.

In conclusion, advocacy and activism are dynamic forces that play essential roles in driving social and political change. Advocacy gives voice to the marginalized, influencing decision-makers and fostering understanding. Activism, with its disruptive nature, demands attention and challenges the status quo. Together, these forces create a powerful synergy, pushing society toward greater justice, equality, and sustainability. As we navigate the complexities of the modern world, the continued commitment to advocacy and activism remains crucial for building a better and more equitable future.

Reflecting on Female Strength

Reflecting on female strength is a profound exploration of the resilience, determination, and multifaceted capabilities that women exhibit in various aspects of life. From historical struggles to contemporary challenges, the tapestry of female strength weaves a compelling narrative that transcends time and cultural boundaries.

Historically, women have faced formidable obstacles, yet their strength has been a driving force in pushing societal boundaries. In the suffragette movement of the late 19th and early 20th centuries, women fought tirelessly for the right to vote, showcasing immense strength in the face of systemic inequality. This struggle laid the foundation for subsequent generations of women to assert their rights and challenge traditional gender norms.

Female strength extends beyond the political sphere into the realm of literature and art. Throughout history, female authors like Jane Austen, Virginia Woolf, and Maya Angelou have used their voices to articulate the complexity of women's experiences. Their narratives not only resonate with readers but also serve as a testament to the strength required to navigate a world that has not always been receptive to female perspectives.

In the contemporary landscape, women continue to demonstrate strength in the face of adversity. The #MeToo movement, for example, has empowered women to speak out against sexual harassment and assault. The collective strength of survivors has sparked a global conversation, challenging societal norms and fostering a sense of solidarity among women.

Furthermore, the professional arena showcases the diverse talents and capabilities of women. From entrepreneurs breaking glass ceilings to scientists making groundbreaking discoveries, women are excelling in fields traditionally dominated by men. The strength required to navigate male-dominated industries is a testament to the resilience and determination ingrained in the female experience.

Motherhood, often overlooked as a source of strength, is a profound aspect of female resilience. The physical and emotional endurance required to nurture and raise a child is unparalleled. Juggling the responsibilities of career and family, many women exemplify strength as they navigate the delicate balance of motherhood.

In the face of health challenges, women demonstrate remarkable strength. From battling chronic illnesses to overcoming reproductive health issues, the female body undergoes tremendous physical strain. The strength required to persevere through these challenges reflects the innate resilience that defines the female experience.

Despite progress, societal expectations and stereotypes still place burdens on women. The pressure to conform to beauty standards, balance career and family, and navigate societal expectations can be overwhelming. Female strength, in this context, lies in the ability to resist conformity and embrace authenticity, challenging the status quo.

Intersectionality adds another layer to the discussion of female strength. Women of different races, ethnicities, sexual orientations, and socio-economic backgrounds face unique challenges. Recognizing and celebrating the strength of women from diverse backgrounds is essential to fostering inclusivity and equality.

It is crucial to acknowledge that female strength is not a monolithic concept. Strength manifests in various forms, and each woman's journey is unique. The collective strength of women, however, creates a powerful force for change and progress.

In conclusion, reflecting on female strength is an exploration of the myriad ways women exhibit resilience, determination, and capability. From historical struggles to contemporary challenges, the strength of women transcends time and cultural boundaries. By recognizing and celebrating female strength, we contribute to a more inclusive and equitable world where the power of women is acknowledged and respected.

Empowering the Future

Empowering the future is an imperative task that transcends individual, societal, and global boundaries. At its core, this concept encapsulates the idea of equipping individuals with the tools, knowledge, and opportunities needed to not only navigate the complexities of the modern world but also to actively shape and contribute to its evolution.

Education stands as a paramount pillar in empowering the future. Beyond the traditional classroom setting, it involves fostering a lifelong learning mindset that encourages adaptability and continuous skill development. The future demands individuals capable of critical thinking, problem-solving, and creativity, attributes that go beyond rote memorization.

Technological advancements play a pivotal role in shaping the trajectory of empowerment. Bridging the digital divide ensures that individuals, regardless of their socio-economic background, have access to information and resources. Digital literacy becomes a key component, enabling people to harness the vast potential of technology for personal and collective growth.

Economic empowerment goes hand in hand with education and technology. Creating inclusive economic systems that provide equal opportunities for all is essential. Entrepreneurship, innovation, and sustainable business practices become catalysts for positive change, unlocking new avenues for growth and prosperity.

Social empowerment involves fostering inclusivity, diversity, and equal representation. Breaking down barriers based on gender, race, or other factors ensures that every individual has a voice and a seat at the table. Empowering marginalized communities contributes not only to their well-being but also to the enrichment of society as a whole.

Environmental stewardship is a critical aspect of empowering the future. Sustainable practices and a heightened awareness of the impact of human activities on the planet are essential. Encouraging eco-friendly lifestyles, conservation efforts, and responsible resource management pave the way for a more sustainable and resilient future.

Global collaboration emerges as a necessity in empowering the future. Complex challenges, such as climate change, pandemics, and socio-economic disparities, require collective action. International cooperation fosters the exchange of ideas, resources, and expertise, creating a synergy that transcends borders and benefits humanity as a whole.

Cultivating emotional intelligence becomes increasingly important in an interconnected world. Empathy, communication skills, and cultural understanding form the bedrock of harmonious relationships, both at the individual and societal levels. Nurturing emotional intelligence equips individuals to navigate diverse perspectives and build bridges across differences.

Political empowerment plays a crucial role in shaping the future trajectory of societies. Transparent and accountable governance structures ensure that the needs and aspirations of the people are represented and addressed. Civic engagement becomes a powerful tool for individuals to actively participate in the decision-making processes that shape their communities.

In the realm of healthcare, empowering the future involves not only advancing medical research and technology but also ensuring universal access to quality healthcare. Prioritizing preventive measures, mental health support, and holistic well-being contributes to a healthier and more resilient population.

Cultural preservation and innovation are integral components of empowerment. Valuing and preserving cultural heritage while embracing innovation fosters a dynamic and rich tapestry of human expression. This intersection allows societies to draw strength from their roots while embracing the possibilities of the future.

In conclusion, empowering the future requires a holistic and multifaceted approach. It involves a commitment to education, technological advancement, economic inclusivity, social justice, environmental sustainability, global collaboration, emotional intelligence, political transparency, healthcare accessibility, and cultural vitality. By addressing these facets, individuals and societies can forge a path towards a future that is not only prosperous but also sustainable, inclusive, and harmonious.

A1 Profiles of Remarkable Women

A1 Profiles of Remarkable Women

In the ever-evolving tapestry of human history, women have played pivotal roles, contributing significantly to various fields and breaking barriers along the way. The A1 Profiles of Remarkable Women showcases the extraordinary achievements, resilience, and impact of women who have left an indelible mark on society. This collection delves into diverse realms, from science and literature to activism and leadership, celebrating the multifaceted brilliance of these exceptional individuals.

One of the luminaries featured in this compilation is Marie Curie, a trailblazing scientist whose groundbreaking research in radioactivity earned her not one but two Nobel Prizes in Physics and Chemistry. Her unwavering dedication to science paved the way for future generations of female scientists, challenging societal norms and redefining the possibilities for women in STEM fields.

Moving beyond the realms of science, the collection also explores the literary prowess of Maya Angelou. Her eloquent words and powerful verses resonate with readers globally, addressing themes of identity, race, and resilience. Angelou's autobiographical work, including the acclaimed "I Know Why the Caged Bird Sings," not only broke literary ground but also became a source of inspiration for individuals navigating their own life challenges.

In the realm of activism, Malala Yousafzai stands out as a beacon of courage and advocacy for girls' education. Surviving a targeted attack by the Taliban, Malala's resilience and unwavering commitment to education for all have made her a symbol of hope and empowerment. Her A1 profile illuminates the impact that one individual, regardless of age or gender, can have in creating positive change on a global scale.

Shifting focus to the world of business and leadership, A1 also highlights the achievements of women like Indra Nooyi, the former CEO of PepsiCo. Nooyi's strategic acumen and leadership skills not only propelled PepsiCo to new heights but also shattered glass ceilings, emphasizing the importance of gender diversity in corporate leadership.

Within the realm of arts and entertainment, the collection features the incomparable Audrey Hepburn. Beyond her iconic film roles, Hepburn's humanitarian efforts and commitment to UNICEF showcase the profound influence artists can wield in promoting positive change beyond the silver screen.

In the field of sports, Serena Williams emerges as a dominant force, redefining tennis and challenging perceptions of women in athletics. Williams' tenacity, skill, and numerous Grand Slam victories have solidified her as one of the greatest athletes of her generation, inspiring countless aspiring athletes to pursue their dreams relentlessly.

The A1 Profiles of Remarkable Women is not just a celebration of individual achievements but a testament to the collective strength and resilience of women throughout history. It serves as a reminder that progress and innovation know no gender, and the contributions of women have been, and continue to be, essential in shaping the world we live in.

This compilation aims to inspire and educate, fostering a deeper appreciation for the diverse and extraordinary accomplishments of women across different fields and cultures. By acknowledging these A1 profiles, we honor the legacy of those who paved the way and empower future generations to reach even greater heights. The remarkable women featured in this collection exemplify the transformative power of passion, perseverance, and the indomitable human spirit.

Potential Growth of a Woman

The potential growth of a woman encompasses a multifaceted journey that spans various aspects of her life. From personal development to professional pursuits, women have the capacity to achieve remarkable growth and make significant contributions to society. This exploration will delve into key areas such as education, career, personal empowerment, and societal impact, shedding light on the myriad ways in which women can unlock their potential and thrive.

Education serves as a cornerstone for the growth of any individual, and women are no exception. Access to quality education empowers women with knowledge, critical thinking skills, and the ability to navigate the complexities of the world. Over the years, strides have been made globally to bridge the gender gap in education, with more women pursuing higher studies and breaking barriers in traditionally male-dominated fields. Recognizing and nurturing the intellectual potential of women lays the groundwork for their holistic development.

In the realm of career and professional growth, women have been challenging stereotypes and glass ceilings. The evolution of workplace dynamics has seen a shift towards recognizing and harnessing the unique skills and perspectives that women bring to the table. Efforts to promote diversity and inclusion have opened up avenues for women to excel in various professions, from STEM (science, technology, engineering, and mathematics) fields to leadership roles in corporate settings. The potential for women to thrive in their careers is amplified when they are given equal opportunities and support to advance.

Personal empowerment plays a pivotal role in the growth of women. Cultivating self-confidence, resilience, and a sense of agency allows women to navigate challenges and pursue their aspirations. Empowerment is not only about individual growth but also extends to fostering a supportive environment where women can uplift one another. Initiatives that promote mentorship, networking, and skill-building contribute to the empowerment of women, enabling them to realize their full potential in both personal and professional spheres.

Societal impact is another dimension of a woman's potential growth. Women have historically played crucial roles in shaping communities and influencing positive change. As leaders, caregivers, and community builders, women contribute to the social fabric in unique ways. Recognizing and valuing the diverse contributions of women in society is essential for creating a more equitable and inclusive world. When women are empowered to lead and participate actively, the ripple effects can lead to broader societal progress.

The potential growth of a woman is intertwined with the broader narrative of gender equality. Advocacy for women's rights, dismantling systemic barriers, and challenging societal norms that limit women's potential are crucial steps towards fostering an environment where women can thrive. By addressing issues such as gender-based violence, unequal access to opportunities, and discriminatory practices, societies can create conditions that enable the holistic growth of women.

In conclusion, the potential growth of a woman is a dynamic and multifaceted journey encompassing education, career, personal empowerment, and societal impact. As women continue to break barriers, challenge stereotypes, and contribute meaningfully to various aspects of life, it is imperative to create a supportive and inclusive environment that recognizes and values their potential. Embracing diversity, promoting equal opportunities, and championing women's rights are integral steps towards unlocking the full potential of women and building a more equitable and vibrant future for all.

Representations in Media

Women's representations in media have evolved over the years, reflecting societal shifts and changing perspectives on gender roles. In the early days of media, women were often portrayed in stereotypical and limiting roles, reinforcing traditional gender norms. However, as society progressed, so did the portrayal of women in various forms of media, including television, film, advertising, and social media.

Historically, women were frequently depicted as passive and dependent on male characters. In early films, they were often cast as damsels in distress or portrayed as nurturing figures. These representations not only reinforced traditional gender roles but also contributed to the perpetuation of harmful stereotypes. As feminism gained momentum in the 20th century, there was a push for more nuanced and empowering portrayals of women in media.

The 1970s and 1980s saw the rise of the women's liberation movement, influencing the portrayal of women in media. Strong, independent female characters began to emerge, challenging conventional stereotypes. Television shows like "The Mary Tyler Moore Show" and "Charlie's Angels" featured women in professional roles, breaking away from the limited options previously presented.

Despite these strides, the media landscape continued to grapple with issues such as objectification and the oversexualization of women. Advertisements often featured unrealistic and idealized images of women, promoting beauty standards that were unattainable for many. This trend persisted in various forms of media, perpetuating harmful beauty ideals and negatively impacting women's self-esteem.

The 21st century brought about a digital revolution, with the rise of social media providing a platform for diverse voices and perspectives. This shift allowed women to reclaim their narratives and challenge traditional representations. The #MeToo movement, for instance, shed light on issues of harassment and abuse within the entertainment industry, prompting a reevaluation of power dynamics and gender representation.

In recent years, there has been a growing awareness of the need for diversity and inclusion in media portrayals. Efforts have been made to showcase a broader spectrum of women, including those from different ethnicities, body types, and backgrounds. This push for diversity aims to break down stereotypes and offer more authentic representations that resonate with a diverse audience.

While progress has been made, challenges persist. Gender-based stereotypes, subtle biases, and unequal opportunities still permeate the media industry. The Bechdel Test, a measure of female representation in fiction, highlights the ongoing disparities in how women are portrayed. Despite improvements, there is a continued need for increased representation behind the scenes, with more women involved in writing, directing, and producing to ensure diverse and authentic storytelling.

The impact of media representation on society cannot be understated. Media plays a crucial role in shaping perceptions and influencing societal norms. The way women are portrayed in media can affect real-world attitudes and behaviors, contributing to either the reinforcement or dismantling of gender stereotypes. Therefore, it is essential for media creators to be conscious of the messages they convey and strive for more inclusive and empowering representations.

In conclusion, the representations of women in media have undergone significant transformations throughout history. From reinforcing traditional gender norms to challenging stereotypes, the evolving portrayal of women reflects broader societal changes. While progress has been made, there is still work to be done to ensure diverse, authentic, and empowering representations of women in all forms of media. The ongoing efforts towards inclusivity and equality will continue to shape the way women are depicted, ultimately influencing societal perceptions and expectations.

Community Building

Community building is a multifaceted process that involves creating connections, fostering collaboration, and nurturing a sense of belonging among individuals. It goes beyond geographical proximity, extending into shared interests, values, and goals. A thriving community is characterized by strong social bonds, effective communication, and mutual support. In this exploration of community building, we'll delve into its importance, key principles, and practical strategies.

At its core, community building addresses the innate human need for connection. In an era dominated by digital interactions, fostering genuine relationships is crucial for combating isolation and building resilient communities. Shared experiences, whether online or offline, create a foundation for trust and understanding. These connections serve as the building blocks for a supportive network that can weather challenges and celebrate successes together.

Understanding the principles of community building is essential for those aiming to create meaningful connections. Open communication lays the groundwork, encouraging individuals to express their thoughts, ideas, and concerns. This transparency builds trust and promotes a sense of inclusivity. Active listening, another fundamental principle, ensures that community members feel heard and valued. This reciprocal exchange fosters a culture of empathy and understanding.

A sense of shared purpose is a powerful catalyst for community building. When individuals unite around a common goal or passion, it creates a cohesive identity that strengthens their connections. Whether it's a local gardening club, an online support group, or a neighborhood association, having a shared purpose provides direction and fuels collective enthusiasm.

Inclusivity is a cornerstone of successful community building. Diverse perspectives contribute to a richer tapestry of ideas and experiences. Embracing diversity promotes tolerance and broadens the community's collective knowledge. By creating an environment where everyone feels welcome regardless of their background, a community becomes more resilient and adaptable to change.

Leadership plays a crucial role in community building. Effective leaders inspire and empower others, fostering a sense of ownership and responsibility within the community. They set a positive tone, model collaborative behavior, and encourage others to contribute their skills and talents. Leadership doesn't necessarily come from a single figurehead; rather, it can emerge from various community members who step up to guide and inspire.

Practical strategies are integral to transforming community-building principles into actionable steps. Hosting regular events, whether in person or online, provides opportunities for individuals to connect and strengthen relationships. Workshops, seminars, and social gatherings centered around shared interests create a platform for learning and collaboration. Utilizing technology can enhance community building in the digital age. Online forums, social media groups, and collaborative platforms facilitate communication and enable members to stay connected beyond physical boundaries. Virtual spaces offer accessibility, allowing individuals with diverse schedules or geographical locations to participate actively.

Community-building initiatives often benefit from a bottom-up approach, empowering individuals to take the lead in organizing activities or projects. This decentralization fosters a sense of ownership, with community members actively contributing to the growth and sustainability of the group.

Promoting volunteerism is another effective strategy for community building. Engaging in collective efforts to address local needs not only benefits the community but also strengthens the bonds among its members. Whether it's organizing a neighborhood cleanup, supporting local charities, or collaborating on a community garden, volunteering creates shared experiences that contribute to a sense of unity.

Celebrating achievements, both big and small, is vital for reinforcing a positive community culture. Recognizing individual contributions and milestones fosters a sense of pride and shared accomplishment. Regularly acknowledging and appreciating the efforts of community members creates a supportive atmosphere that encourages continued engagement.

In conclusion, community building is a dynamic and ongoing process that involves cultivating connections, fostering inclusivity, and promoting shared purpose. By embracing these principles and implementing practical strategies, individuals can contribute to the creation of resilient, supportive communities. Whether in physical neighborhoods or virtual spaces, the power of community building lies in its ability to enrich lives, create lasting connections, and positively impact society as a whole.

Changing Dynamics

Changing dynamics is a constant in the fabric of life, permeating various aspects of our existence. Whether in the realms of technology, society, or personal relationships, the only certainty is change. This fluidity challenges our adaptability, forcing us to navigate through an ever-evolving landscape.

In the realm of technology, the pace of change is staggering. Advancements that once took decades are now compressed into mere years. The dynamics of industries are transformed as emerging technologies disrupt established norms. Artificial Intelligence, blockchain, and quantum computing are not just buzzwords but catalysts reshaping the very foundation of how we live and work.

Societal dynamics mirror the shifting sands of technological progress. Cultural norms, once deeply rooted, now face seismic shifts. The definition of success, the concept of family, and the perception of identity are all in a state of flux. Gender roles, long confined to traditional stereotypes, are experiencing a profound transformation, challenging age-old paradigms and fostering a more inclusive society.

Economic dynamics are also subject to change. Globalization, once seen as an unstoppable force, is now met with skepticism. Trade alliances are reevaluated, and the balance of economic power is shifting. The rise of new economic players and the decline of established giants create a dynamic economic landscape, influencing markets and trade relations worldwide.

In the workplace, the dynamics of employment are undergoing a metamorphosis. Remote work, once a rare privilege, is now a mainstream practice. The traditional 9-to-5 model is giving way to flexible schedules and a focus on results rather than hours spent in the office. The gig economy is flourishing, offering both opportunities and challenges as it redefines the employer-employee relationship.

Environmental concerns introduce a new layer to changing dynamics. Climate change is not a distant threat but a present reality, influencing policies, industries, and individual choices. The dynamics of resource consumption and conservation are reexamined as the world grapples with the urgent need for sustainable practices.

On a personal level, changing dynamics manifest in relationships. The dynamics of friendships, family ties, and romantic connections evolve over time. Communication, influenced by technology, takes on new forms, impacting the way we relate to one another. The definition of personal success and fulfillment undergoes introspection, reshaping life goals and priorities.

Education, a cornerstone of societal progress, is not immune to changing dynamics. The traditional classroom model is being augmented by online learning platforms, offering accessibility and flexibility. Lifelong learning becomes a necessity in a world where skills become obsolete at an unprecedented rate.

Amidst these shifting dynamics, resilience and adaptability emerge as crucial traits. Navigating change requires a willingness to embrace uncertainty and a commitment to continuous learning. The ability to unlearn and relearn becomes a valuable skill as old paradigms give way to new possibilities.

However, changing dynamics also bring challenges. Resistance to change, fear of the unknown, and the inertia of established systems can impede progress. Striking a balance between preserving the essence of what is valuable and embracing the opportunities presented by change is a delicate task.

In conclusion, changing dynamics are an intrinsic part of the human experience. From the technological revolution reshaping industries to the societal shifts transforming cultural norms, the only constant is change. Navigating this ever-evolving landscape requires adaptability, resilience, and a willingness to embrace the unknown. As we stand on the precipice of the future, the ability to navigate changing dynamics will be a defining factor in shaping a thriving and sustainable world.

Conclusion

In conclusion, the might of a woman is a formidable force that permeates every facet of human existence. From the nurturing warmth of a mother to the unyielding determination of a leader, women contribute significantly to the tapestry of our world. In examining the various dimensions of this might, it becomes evident that women possess a unique strength rooted in resilience, compassion, and the ability to overcome adversity.
One of the defining aspects of a woman's might is her resilience. Throughout history, women have faced countless challenges, societal expectations, and systemic barriers. Despite these hurdles, they have displayed an indomitable spirit, bouncing back from setbacks and standing tall in the face of adversity. Whether it be in personal or professional realms, the ability to adapt and persevere underscores the might of a woman.

Moreover, the might of a woman is intricately woven with compassion. Women often serve as the emotional backbone of families and communities, offering solace, empathy, and understanding. This nurturing instinct extends beyond familial bonds, influencing workplaces, social circles, and global movements. The capacity for compassion enables women to bridge gaps, foster connections, and create environments that thrive on empathy.

The empowerment of women is a testament to their might, as societies recognize the importance of tapping into the full potential of their female populations. In education, business, politics, and various fields, women continue to break barriers and shatter glass ceilings. The might of a woman is not confined to any particular sector but permeates every sphere of human activity, contributing to a more equitable and inclusive world.
In leadership, women bring a unique set of qualities that enrich decision-making processes. Collaborative, inclusive, and emotionally intelligent leadership styles are hallmarks of many successful women leaders. The might of a woman in positions of influence has the power to reshape organizational cultures and societal norms, fostering environments that value diversity and embrace a multiplicity of perspectives.
Furthermore, the might of a woman is evident in her ability to inspire and effect change on a global scale. From activists advocating for gender equality to scientists making groundbreaking discoveries, women contribute significantly to the advancement of humanity. Their voices resonate in movements that strive for justice, equality, and a better world. The ripple effect of their actions extends far beyond individual achievements, creating a legacy of empowerment for generations to come.
In the realm of creativity and innovation, the might of a woman shines brightly. Countless women have left an indelible mark in literature, art, science, and technology. Their creativity knows no bounds, and their contributions continue to shape the cultural and intellectual landscape of our world. Recognizing and celebrating these achievements amplifies the importance of fostering environments that encourage the exploration of diverse talents and perspectives.

In conclusion, the might of a woman is a dynamic force that encompasses resilience, compassion, leadership, empowerment, and creativity. It is not a singular characteristic but a tapestry of qualities that collectively contribute to the betterment of humanity. As societies continue to evolve, recognizing and harnessing the full potential of women is not just a matter of equality but a strategic imperative for a more harmonious and prosperous world.

Embracing the might of a woman is not merely a choice; it is an acknowledgment of the rich and multifaceted contributions that women make to the intricate mosaic of human existence.